NOW THAT'S WHAT I CALL

THE TRUTH

BY

KAY SUTHERLAND

kaysutherlandauthor.co.uk

Love is the key!

First Published in the United Kingdom by
Kay Sutherland August 2017

Copyright © 2017 Kay Sutherland

First edition
ISBN 9781522063360
Published by Kay Sutherland

Contents

Acknowledgements

I would like to thank…

> …my mum and her partner for supporting me financially in the aftermath.

> ..my beautiful daughter for being the reason I kept putting one foot in front of the other.

> ..my many wonderful friends for their never-ending support. Your kind words, knowledge and collective shoulder to cry on have been phenomenal. I will always appreciate your kindness.

> …my wonderful friend and proof reader who has spent many hours pouring over these pages.

And finally, a huge 'Thank you' to my friend who inspired me to write this book.

You all have a very special place in my heart

Forward

Perhaps you have been drawn to this book by the front cover or maybe you are desperately reaching out for some validation of the crazy experiences you are having with your current partner. If you are in a relationship with a narcissist you are probably feeling very isolated and if the narcissist has been successful in their campaign, you may be blaming yourself. A subtle grinding down of your sense of self and self-worth is a sure sign of a toxic relationship. Confusion is another red flag of an unhealthy relationship. Kay describes red flags (what to look out for) and various personality disordered traits. There are many and I encourage you to boldly step forward on this journey of discovery. I guarantee your perception of how the world works will be enlightening and valuable for your future, both in your personal and professional life.

I have known Kay for two years and met her when she was coming to the end of her relationship with a narcissist. Like myself, she hadn't considered that she was dealing with a personality-disordered person. This book demonstrates how, from the depths of utter despair, through learning and researching about narcissism, Kay freed herself to a more fulfilling life and a deeper connection with herself. Kay is passionate about sharing her message and experience so others may be spared the pain she endured. Kay learned that only by loving herself could she free herself from the effects of her tortuous relationship.

You will come to realise that it is not your fault that you are involved with a narcissist and there is hope for a peaceful and fulfilling future. I commend you in picking up this book, and encourage you to pursue your own research. This new insight will strengthen and enlighten you.

For indeed you must be a loving, compassionate and forgiving person if you find yourself involved with a personality-disordered person.

Hannah

Preface

I am the survivor of an abusive relationship with a Narcissistic Sociopath. Eighteen months after freeing myself from his grip my life is much improved but I'm still in recovery. I decided to write my story to help overcome the debilitating effects of that relationship. At first it was just about helping me to heal, but then a friend who had also suffered badly at the hands of a narcissistic sociopath persuaded me to publish my story to help others who have experienced similar abuse to understand a little more about this type of personality disorder.

In these pages I describe how I first met my abuser, how he wormed his way into my life, how he abused me and how he extracted everything he wanted from me. I also describe how his dysfunctional behaviour affected me psychologically during the time we were together and the difficulties I have faced in trying to recover and live a normal life again.

This is a true story. It contains details of what actually happened to me; only the names have been changed for privacy.

I'm not claiming to be an expert on narcissism but I have researched extensively in search of answers by reading a wide variety of books and making full use of the many resources on the Internet. I've also attended formal support groups and am a member of several informal Internet groups.

I hope that this book will help you understand what has happened if you've been unfortunate and suffered at the hands of a narcissist or know someone who has been on the receiving end of narcissistic abuse.

Kay Sutherland
August 2017

Chapter One

We met on a self-development/business course. I was looking to expand my business and trying everything I could to get out of my comfort zone, to push the limits and make a breakthrough. However, I was struggling to come to terms with the death of my Grandad and a close friend. I was also getting over the effects of being bullied due to jealousy over the success I'd had in my business in a short period of time.

Still I was in a fantastic position, my business was still doing well, I had great friends, was financially free and after years of therapy, I really felt I had my head screwed on properly. People I worked alongside respected me. I had 4 or 5 holidays a year and life was really amazing. My business gave me so much freedom and I felt truly grateful.

Many people who knew me said I would light up the room when I walked in. I was so positive and happy despite the difficulties. I practised mindfulness and meditation and looked for the best in everyone and everything.

The course leader asked us to sit in small groups; I sat near the front. I noticed a guy sitting directly behind me; he was charming and chatty. I could tell he wasn't English; he was tall and slim with very dark, sleeked back hair and designer stubble around his strong jawline. I'd seen him earlier swaggering around the room in his Ralph Lauren designer shirt like he owned the place and he clearly had a great deal of confidence.

We started chatting and exchanged our stories, discussed why we were on the course and what we were hoping to achieve. He told me he was called Antonio, that he was Italian and lived in London. He said that a friend had recommended the event and that he was looking for inspiration to expand his many businesses. He also explained he had brought a friend called Paul along to the event. Paul was miserable and needed something to change his energy after many failed attempts at trying to set up his own business and relationship problems. I found this man's honesty very refreshing and liked his confidence. I enjoyed our conversation.

I explained to Antonio that I was looking to expand my business by finding people with drive and ambition who were willing to invest their time in it.

A few moments later Antonio shouted across the room, waving his arms around frantically. A tall stocky man with ginger hair and striking blue eyes, who was clearly angry and appeared depressed, wandered over. "What?" he said. He looked at me like I was the devil. Antonio told the man that he needed to listen to what I had to say. "This is perfect for you," Antonio said with excitement in his tone. " This lady is willing to help you and it won't cost anything."

The stocky man clearly had his mind on other things and didn't want to talk to me. Antonio took my business card and told the man to take one too.

After the weekend the stocky man rang me. "Hi it's me, Paul. I met you on the business course. Is it a good time? I need help getting started with this business," he said.

"Of course," I said, "anything I can do to help. Just ask."

Paul told me he was a recovering heroin addict and had been clean for 11 years. He had taken the drug from being 11 years old. He told me about his shady past including stealing cars, burglary and physical assault. He assured me that he had changed and wanted my help to start in the business because he thought that would help him stay on the straight and narrow.

He went on to tell me about his abusive childhood, addict parents and abusive partners. He droned on about how he had been mistreated by his last partner who was very abusive, how upset he was about finding sexually explicit photos of her with another man and how he was struggling to cope. Paul went on to tell me about lots of other disasters that he had experienced. I started to feel sorry for him and thought he needed someone to talk to. I fell for his sob stories and wanted to help him.

We spoke night after night. I was his therapist. Paul was very angry about his life; angry that he had to work for a living, angry about regularly being rained off from his job in the building trade and the effect that had on his income. He had two young children, Faye aged 10 and Belle who was 5 years old. The children had different mothers who were both heroin addicts and always very demanding of him.

It seemed Paul was angry about everything; he was so miserable, obsessive, very unhappy with his life and at odds with himself.

Poor him! I felt so sorry for him, poor man. "He's only trying to turn his life around," I thought. I fell for his sob stories and wanted to help him get back on his feet.

Eventually we got into a relationship, I'll explain how later on. For months when we went out he'd say, "Aaahhh, I've no cash. I'll have to pay you back later." I'd say "Okay, no worries," and pay the bill. I paid for everything. I even paid for days out with his children when I went to visit him each fortnight. He expected it and he would often order something while we were out together and then walk away saying, "You have the cash, don't you?" or "Just get it on your card for now."

Each alternate weekend Paul would travel from Devon to see me in Birmingham but always giving me conditions. "I'll come over providing you give me a massage," he'd say. "I'll come over providing you do XY & Z for me."

It was all about him! Everything was but I was blind, I just couldn't see what was going on.

Chapter Two

When I met Paul he had nothing. He couldn't pay his bills, hated work and was always being laid off. He learnt his trade while he'd been in prison on one of the nine occasions he told me about.

I knew he wasn't a good person but I ignored my inner voice and wanted to believe there was good in him. I wanted to help him change his life for the better.

Paul had so many sob stories. His mum was an addict, all his family members were addicts and numerous girlfriends had been unfaithful to him; so many traumas in his life. My heart went out to him and how he had beaten his heroin addiction inspired me. "How can anyone ever come out the other side from something so awful," I thought.

I was in a bad place myself following agonising months of being tormented by bullies from within my business network. They told lies, spread false rumours, ingratiated themselves with my friends so they could try to discredit me with half-truth's, abused me, were very aggressive, damaged my property and turned my support in the business against me. All because I'd been very successful! Sheer jealousy! I hadn't been accustomed to this type of behaviour and it played havoc with my emotions. The ringleader was called Beryl. We had been good friends but now she took great pleasure in telling me stories about people I knew and how they were calling me names behind my back. According to her they even disliked me because of my hairstyle. She had previously confided in me about the struggles she had in keeping friendships with women for longer than three years. Looking back I can see why?

The venomous bullies had isolated me from so many people. Even people I thought were my friends became two faced, unsupportive and sat on the fence. That hurt so much; I couldn't understand how people who were supposed to be my friends could believe those untruths and turn against me? They didn't have a clue about how they too had been manipulated.

I desperately needed support and found comfort in having big, burly Paul in my life. We talked on the phone for hours and hours discussing his painful experiences and the effect that my tormentors were having on me. Paul complained about everything and everyone. As far as he was concerned all women were slags and couldn't be trusted. He told me he hated his mother who was also a recovering heroin addict, and apparently hadn't spoken to him for many years.

I loved our friendship and felt protected. Paul said "The bullies won't come near you with me about. I'll smash their faces in." Just what I needed! Support. Back-up. A bodyguard. Someone to stand up for me - at last!

I was hurting and vulnerable. My guard was down and he saw my emotional frailty as an opportunity. Paul took advantage, abused my good nature, formed a fake relationship with me and wheedled his way into my life.

After speaking on the phone each night for several months Paul suggested coming over to spend some time with me to learn everything about the business. As he didn't have much money for a hotel he asked if he could stay with me. I was extremely focused and as far as I was concerned it was all about the business. Paul seemed keen to learn and I was happy to help. I felt we had a great, supportive friendship and told him that I had a spare room and he was welcome to stay for a couple of nights. "We're only friends helping each other after all," I thought. So we decided he would come and stay with me for a weekend and I'd teach him everything I knew about the business.

Paul told me that he would be arriving in time for an evening meal around 7pm but he turned up sometime after 11pm. No phone call to say he'd be late and when he arrived he made some excuse about being unable to set off when he planned as Faye wanted him to get a Chinese takeaway for her. I remember thinking, "How disrespectful."

I was sleepy by the time he arrived and was staggered when I answered the door and saw how many bags he had brought. I thought he was moving in!

The food that I had carefully prepared was more than ready and almost in the dog by that time in the evening. "I don't fancy a big meal now, I'll just have a sandwich instead," Paul said. "Have you any crisps?"

Paul followed me into the kitchen. I noticed that he immediately seemed at home and very comfortable. I noticed how he scanned the room. I also noticed how he scanned me up and down. His eyes were all over the place. I remember thinking "Just keep focused on the business. That's what you're here for, young man." Incidentally Paul was 7 years younger than me.

While Paul was making himself at home and putting his feet up I made a warm drink for both of us. He ate his sandwich and crisps and then said he needed chocolate and milk. He drank almost a pint of milk and demolished my biscuit barrel.

We sat chatting until the early hours of the morning. He sat on one sofa and I sat on another. It was exciting; making plans for the business and listening to his grandiose ideas.

Paul seemed really keen to learn and was very confident in himself. I thought, "He's going to be perfect for this type of business."

I'd made a very clear structure for the weekend and planned what we needed to cover to help him get started. I'd spent a week preparing the topics we needed to cover.

I lost track of time and when I looked at the clock I was surprised to see it was 2.30am. "Right," I said, "I need to go to bed. I'll have breakfast ready for 9.30 and we need to start work at 10 o'clock. We have a lot to cover."

Paul followed me upstairs. I showed him to his room then went to the bathroom to put my pyjamas on.

We continued to chat about this and that, mainly about the business at that point. He sat on the step just outside my bedroom. I was already in bed with my pyjamas and dressing gown on.

"If you want to sit on the sofa in my room, that's ok," I said. He quickly moved and sat on the sofa at the bottom of my bed.

Snuggled under the quilt, I was secretly excited at the thought of growth and new energy in the business. Paul had such grandiose ideas and really seemed excited about achieving them.

Paul continued to tell me story after story. I felt I could have stayed up and listened to him all night but I was getting sleepier by the minute. Soon my eyes were rolling and I eventually drifted off into a deep sleep around 3am.

I stress that it was a deep sleep as I'm usually a very light sleeper!

I half-woke just after 4am feeling very drowsy and strangely confused to find this man, my friend, my bodyguard, helping himself to my body. I remember asking Paul, "What are you doing?" He said, "You know I like you."

Seconds after I stirred, he had finished. He'd got what he wanted.

I woke properly at 8.30am wondering what the hell had happened. How did he get my dressing gown and pyjamas off without me stirring? How did he take advantage of my body without me waking? Why was I in such a sleepy state? Why was I so confused? Usually if the cat climbs on me while I'm asleep I'll wake up and be quite alert. I really don't understand what happened that night but he was my friend, my bodyguard. I trusted him and he said he would protect me.

Over breakfast I told him, "That wasn't very professional." I joked saying, "I'd rather be awake." I asked Paul what he was thinking. "I don't do one-night stands," I said. "Do you want a relationship with me?"

Paul told me he wasn't ready for another relationship. He told me his ex was so deceitful and had hurt him so much that he wouldn't be able to have another relationship for a long time. "When I'm ready for another relationship I want it to be with you," he said.

That day I struggled to focus. I felt confused, used and had mixed feelings about my friend. Despite his behaviour the previous night, I still wanted to help Paul; I wanted to help him improve his life. But I was also thinking that he could help me get my business back on track and overcome the downturn that occurred during the bullying phase. It would be a two-way thing; we could help each other.

Paul envied my life-style. I had a great work/life balance, freedom from the 9-5 routine, financial security and the respect of my colleagues and friends. He said he'd never had those things and wanted me to help him achieve them.

Over the weekend he gave me lots of hugs and frequently thanked me for helping him. He said, "No one's ever cared before."

By the time Paul was due to leave all the confusion seemed to have evaporated from my mind. What happened on the night he arrived was a distant memory.

Paul and I started to see each other regularly every week or two. As we lived a few hours drive from each other it wasn't always possible to get together but we spoke on the phone at least 4 times every day.

When we were together we'd go out for meals and spend hours and hours chatting like any normal couple would.

Then one day Paul came on to me again. I said, "Well are we together now? Are we in a relationship? You can't have your cake and eat it."

"Well, kind of," was his reply.

Chapter Three

We became closer and closer, my bodyguard and I. Very soon I started to feel stronger, more supported. I loved having Paul around. He was my protector. Paul had a menacing stare that I found quite reassuring in a strange way. He could be quite intimidating but was also strangely enticing and intimate at the same time.

We started spending as much time together as we could. When we weren't together Paul would ring me constantly and quiz me about my whereabouts and who I was with, whether I'd had any phone calls that day and what we'd talked about. Questions, questions, and more questions, often before I'd had a chance to say 'Hello'. I thought he was being extremely nosey and often felt that I was being interrogated but I humoured him and answered his questions honestly.

The fortnightly commute to visit him was hard; it was a long, tiring journey that became so monotonous after a while. After a holiday away together, we decided that Paul should move in with me. "No more bullies", I thought. "I'm in a relationship now. No one will threaten me with him about."

Because he hated his work Paul decided not to look for another job, instead he would take time out. I'd been very successful in my business so he knew I could support the both of us. We could also afford to keep on with the rental of his flat and have his children stay there with us on the weekends when he had access to them.

Then one day when we were out visiting, one of Paul's friends asked, "What are you going to do for work now?" Paul answered, "No need to work. I have my sugar mummy now." I was furious. He had just walked into my life and assumed that I was going to keep him, that he was entitled to share everything I had; my home, my car, my money, my friends.

On a typical day I'd get up and he'd stay in bed. I'd get some work done and around lunchtime he'd shout from the bed, "Sausage sandwich. Yes please my love." I was so blinded by the sweet names Paul would call me when he wanted something that I'd rush to prepare his late breakfast.

"Run me a bath please my darling," he would say. "Ah yes, of course," I'd reply as though it was my duty to be his servant. When Paul had a bath he'd often ask me to wash his hair and wash him down. Sometimes he'd curl up in a ball in the bath and want to be stroked. Paul would stand up in the bath and often shout for me to fetch a towel. He'd stretch out his arms and wait for me to wrap him in the bath towel and put another on the floor at his feet.

He needed mothering like a small child; everything as he demanded. He must have felt like a king. I certainly treated him like one.

Paul would update his social media, and then announce he was off to the gym. "Leg day," he would say. "OK, what time will you be back?" I'd ask. "I'm not sure yet, as long as it takes," would be his reply. He would often go to the gym two or three times a day.

Paul would come home hours later hungry, very hungry, and eat everything in sight. I could barely keep up with the food bill. Sometimes he would eat 4 or 5 meals a day and often have a huge bowl of fruit up to 4 or 5 times a day as well. The pressure of paying for it all stressed me so much but I never showed it. I just continued to be his faithful servant, looking after his every need.

Every day Paul would spend hours on the phone talking to his family, watching TV or YouTube and updating his social media. He'd share details of the incredible life of freedom and rich comfort that he had found. He'd often share pictures of his breakfast in bed or food that I had lovingly prepared for him. He would also go on my social media and post things that looked as though they were from me; he had all my passwords so I had no privacy. Paul constantly played on my phone as much as he did on his own and I often felt that he was checking up on me. I'd think, "This is too much." But then I'd feel sorry for him again. I made excuses for his paranoia.

Occasionally midweek Paul would say, "I deserve a break, let's go shopping." What he really meant was, "I want to go shopping and I expect you to buy me what I want." At the shops we'd go looking for clothes for him. He often couldn't decide on the colour or style so, of course, if it had a designer label he would want to have one of each. He always pushed my boundaries, taking liberties with my good nature. On one occasion I recall very clearly that he got all the shop staff involved because he couldn't decide on the colour or design he wanted. They were all helping and giving him different garments to try. He used me like a clothes rack; there I was holding all the items he wanted me to purchase for him. The staff talked to me but all attention was on him. He was keeping everyone waiting and when he finally came out of the dressing room he said, "Yes, I'll have all of them." He briefly looked my way and said, so everyone could hear, "You have the money." He just walked away from the cash desk and left me to pay. I remember feeling annoyed by his attitude, the way he felt entitled to buy everything he wanted and just assumed I would pay. He'd not worked for months and I was spending a fortune on things for him.

After shopping we would go for a meal. Paul would always over indulge, spending 2 or 3 times more on his meal than I did on mine. He would often have a starter, two main courses and a dessert washed down with 2 or 3 cold drinks and at least 2 coffees afterwards. He would sit and gorge on his food like he'd never eaten before; his heavy body slouched over his food with his arms out wide covering the table. Paul was such a glutton, always eyeing up my food too. I would often sit and pray his food came out from the kitchen before mine. If mine came first he'd start on my meal whilst waiting for his own. Even after his food had arrived he would often stick his fork in my food too. I repeatedly asked him not to steal from my plate and pointed out that I was hungry too but he took no notice. Paul didn't care about what I said or how I felt about his uncouth behaviour which showed us up in public. Everything was about Paul, what he wanted there and then. As soon as we finished our meal, sometimes even before I finished mine, he would make his way to the door leaving me to settle the bill. At other times when the bill arrived he would become pre-occupied with his phone or just step outside the building to make a call.

Paul was obsessed with money, my money. His world revolved around it. He would ask me every couple of weeks how much I had in the bank and he often asked how much my assets were worth. He couldn't spend my money fast enough but would save everything that was his. Every day he would get out his note pad and pencil and write down every penny he had. He would count it meticulously, placing the coins in piles. It wasn't long before he persuaded me to transfer my savings account into our joint names. He always took me to the bank to draw out when he wanted a large amount; he would sit in the chair opposite the cashier waiting patiently as I withdrew my hard earned cash. It made me feel uncomfortable, even sick to my stomach. I felt something wasn't right each time I handed him another fat A5 envelope stuffed with my money.

Whenever I tried to explain to Paul that I was concerned about the frequent trips to the bank, that the money wouldn't last forever, how my back-up plan was disappearing all too quickly, how I was feeling really uncomfortable about the situation, he always had the words to turn it around and against me, often making me feel guilty. He would say things like, "Are we together or not?" or "I'm trying to make a future for us." "Is it your money or ours?" "Why do you want to keep it all for yourself." All these statements and more made me feel that I was failing him, that I was being selfish and unkind. Parting with my money hurt me deeply but his words cut me even deeper so I always backed down.

There was no limit to the liberties Paul took. I would beat myself up about the situation. I'd wonder how I'd allowed myself to get so tangled up with him and why I continued to put up with his terrible behaviour? Then I'd think about the hard life he had endured and feel sorry for him again. "He deserves a break," I'd think to myself. "If I give him a chance he'll come good." Oh, how I deluded myself.

At the time I didn't understand why I had allowed it to go on. I couldn't begin to explain it to myself so I certainly couldn't explain it to anyone else. It was all so bizarre.

I recall one evening going out with Paul's parents for a meal. We'd been seeing each other about 5 months at the time. Paul stared at his phone while his parents and I chatted. When his phone lost its charge he asked to use mine. "OK, but don't go phoning Australia," I joked. I knew he would be on Facebook; he was obsessed with it and couldn't go for longer than 15 minutes without checking in. The food arrived and Paul quickly passed my phone back to me. I put

21

it back in my bag without looking at it. Later in the evening I nipped to the bathroom and got my phone out to send a message to a friend. I realised that Facebook was still logged in to his account and couldn't resist having a look. I saw messages from two girls who worked with me; I didn't know that he was connected to them. I'd trained them in the business and supported them. "Why is he messaging them?" I wondered.

I opened one message that Paul had sent. It said, "Was lovely meeting you. If you need any advice contact me anytime. You're very attractive and I can see you want nice things in life." The reply was, "Thank you so much. I need advice on what to do with my bathroom lol. I'm in the middle of doing my house up and yes I'd like to set some goals and earn some real money." Paul replied, "I'm a decorator. I'll come over and help you if you like. I can help you set your goals. I earn over £4,000 per week."

"What utter tripe!" I fumed. "He's not a decorator. He's new to this business and hasn't really got a clue!" At that time he wasn't earning £400 a month let alone £4,000 a week. I could feel the blood pumping in my neck. I was shocked to realise that he was trying to get closer to this woman, my friend.

I felt the need to open the second message. It was similar. "Hi you're going to do really well in this business. You're so attractive, how old are you? Did you find me attractive? What did you think when you opened the door? Do you have a boyfriend?" I carried on reading to find the girls reply. "Thank you. I'm really excited. I'm 28 and I don't have a boyfriend. It's complicated and yes you are attractive too. Looking forward to seeing you again." I couldn't believe the words I saw. I read on to find he'd sent pictures of himself half naked, and pretended that he'd sent them accidentally. She'd sent photos of herself in return.

From the beginning Paul had said he needed to take things very slowly and didn't think our relationship should be public knowledge; it wasn't anyone else's business and he wanted to keep me to himself. He told me I was like a guardian angel that had come into his life. He told me no one had ever cared so much. It felt good to share my life and help someone who had been through hell. I now loved and trusted him but what was he doing sending such messages to my colleagues?

I felt betrayed and let down. But as I'd invested so much time and money in Paul I resolved to persevere with our relationship.

Paul had told me that he was very close to his siblings despite them all being dysfunctional and they were all very protective of each other. I recall going to meet one of his sister's for the first time. She invited us in and offered us tea but barely looked at us. All of a sudden she stood up and started screaming at Paul saying how she didn't like either of us because we were too positive. "You aren't normal," she screamed. "Get out of my house." Paul told the rest of his family what had happened and they all agreed she was a psychopath. Over time I realised that all the family members were calling each other. They would block one another for a few months. Then all of a sudden they would be best friends again. I'd never known anything like it and often wondered how they all kept track of who they were or weren't speaking to.

Paul told me that he had struggled with all his relationships. From what he said and did I could clearly see there were no boundaries or defining line between our relationship and any

23

of his other relationships. Boundaries? There just weren't any! He would treat his mum, his sister and daughter Faye in just the same way as he treated me. Paul would tickle me so hard it would hurt; it clearly excited him and he would get an erection. He also tickled his sister and daughter in the same way. "Will he get an erection with them too?" I wondered. I strongly suspect that, yes, he would!

I remember one time at his youngest sister's house. She was working in the kitchen and Paul was standing over her, touching her, teasing her and staring at her in the same strange way he did with many other women while we were out and about. It was strangely intimate.

He often behaved with other women in ways normally reserved for times with a partner. I was only too aware of how he would become excited when he behaved in the same way with me and I often asked him if he thought it was normal to behave that way with other women, especially his sister and daughter. Paul would tell me to "Ssshhhhh." It made me feel uneasy, as though I had to fight for his affection.

At weekends, when we had his two children with us Paul would often sit on the sofa with Faye and watch a film on television. They would stroke and caress each other; with one hand she would stroke his hair and neck and she would stroke his inner thigh with the other. They would be looking at each other as though they were about to make love.

I knew this wasn't normal behaviour and repeatedly told him it wasn't healthy, that Faye needed to have proper boundaries for her own healthy development. I explained to Paul that she was giving him what she thought he wanted; she was looking after his perceived needs. I was conscious that she would become co-dependent on him in an unhealthy way. I was trying to protect her but Paul turned my words against me, accused me of being jealous and told me to keep my nose out. But I knew that sort of behaviour between father and daughter was totally inappropriate.

He wanted attention and so did she, stroking and massaging each other at every opportunity. She often sent him videos of herself and Paul spent hours watching them. I could see she wanted all his attention and I'll never forget seeing the most disturbing video of all in which she licked a sharp knife up and down the full length of the blade with her tongue. Paul found it highly entertaining and when he saw my discomfort he accused me I of being sick for suggesting anything improper. "It's just the love of a daughter for her father," he insisted.

It was true; I was sick; sick of their behaviour. It was making me ill. When I saw or even thought about what the two of them were doing my stomach would churn, my head would ache and I'd get a lump in my throat. I chatted about it endlessly with friends hoping to find a solution. Paul knew I was on his case about his improper behaviour but became very defensive when I tried to discuss the importance of putting healthy boundaries in place.

One night they went across the road to the shop for chocolate. I was doing some jobs around the house and wasn't taking much notice of what they were doing. I remember walking in the room to hear Paul say, "Be careful, and don't get that chocolate on the sofa." Faye replied, "No daddy, I won't." She looked at him in a really manipulative yet flirtatious way. She had the same gluttonous habits as her father and as she devoured the chocolate she spilled bits all over the place. She was laying full stretch on top of Paul. She had one arm around his neck and her legs were entwined with his. He was wearing only tracksuit pants and his naked chest was on show. I looked over to see the ten-year-old licking chocolate crumbs off his naked chest as they stared into each other's eyes and lay there laughing. My stomach churned and I felt sick.

At every opportunity they would sit and stare at each other like love struck teenagers. I remember one time when we went to a theme park and they literally couldn't leave each other alone. They were constantly touching and stroking each other. I remember feeling concerned about Belle being left out but also was conscious of what the on-lookers were thinking. When we took the children out for meals Faye would dash to sit opposite her father and would hold his hands across the table. She would stare lovingly into his eyes and he would stare into hers as though there was no one else in the room.

I tried to make him understand just how unhealthy his behaviour was; how inappropriate it was for father and daughter to sleep in the same bed; how Social Services would react if they became aware; how he could be prosecuted and locked up. He replied very aggressively, " It's no one else's business! I can do whatever the hell I like with my own child." He tried to justify his actions by blaming her mother for abandoning her and said that was why she needed so much attention. What absolute nonsense!

Paul admitted he was obsessed with Faye; she was his addiction – replacing the heroin.

I often felt confused by the whole situation and mentioned it to a friend. She had been doing some research and explained it was 'Emotional Incest' and I started to read up on the subject. "Wow," I thought, "This explains it all." That was a 'light bulb' moment for me. I thought that I finally understood what was going on and I could really help Paul to build a healthy relationship with his daughter. When I explained my findings to him he was initially in denial and said I was talking rubbish. Then he threatened to fall out with me if I ever mentioned it to him again or to anyone else.

I was bursting with all this newly found information; I couldn't help it. I needed to use it somehow and kept dropping hints here and there. I bought books on the subject and continued to spend hours researching. A few weeks later he admitted it. "You're right, you're right about all of it," he said. He admitted to the emotional incest and the dysfunction within his family. "It's not going to be overnight but I see that I need to make changes," he said. "You need to be patient."

All he did was give me hope; I was hanging on by a thread.

Looking back, I feel very sad that Faye had to go through that. She was an extremely obnoxious, entitled child but he abused her. She was clearly a supply, merely a puppet to serve him and his dysfunctional mind.

It was a strange relationship between Paul and Faye. Much of the time I thought she was in control of him but, looking back, I can see that she wasn't in control at all; she was just trying to get control whenever she could. Like the time Paul said he was going vegan; he wanted to be healthy and went on a strict diet of fruit and vegetable for a couple of months. One evening Faye decided she didn't want him to be vegan and started crying, saying that she would fall out with him if he didn't eat meat. So he gave in and started to eat meat again. It was so dysfunctional.

On another occasion Paul asked me to massage his back. Faye came into the room. She was clearly very jealous. "Get off. It's my turn," she said aggressively. I didn't move. I

27

carried on with the massage feeling that I'd been scorned, uncomfortable in her presence. She was clearly very angry because I'd ignored her command. Faye climbed on top of him and he started groaning with delight. He was in his element; two of his supplies pandering to his every need.

Belle stood back quietly taking it all in, the abnormality of it all. So many nights I worried about this young innocent child. Paul always ignored and neglected her, starved her of paternal love and attention. She was the underdog. My heart ached for her. I wished that Paul would sit up and take notice of her. She was always staring up at him with big brown eyes, waiting patiently for any signs of recognition. They never came. Belle was a delightful child, a pleasure to be around. I spent so much time trying to teach Paul how to show love for this little one but nothing changed, he continued to ignore her. Everyone, including his family, could clearly see that she was the underdog and it made me so sad to see such a lovely loving child treated so badly. If both children were with him he would only interact with Faye. I tried my hardest to change that by showing them how to take turns, playing board games, helping them to interact in a healthy way.

Paul's excuse for ignoring Belle was that her mother had trapped him by saying she was on the pill when she wasn't. He resented both mother and child. Paul had been in a relationship with another woman at the time and he continued to sleep with both of them. (I found out later he'd kept on sleeping with them both while he was in the relationship with me too.) We were all just supplies to him. He was keeping the door open to all of us. I was just one of the many feeding his need for adoration and attention.

Somehow he had triangulated all of us. All my focus was on him and the dysfunction in which I'd become enmeshed. He would play us all off against each other trying to make us all jealous. It was like I was in competition with his ex-girlfriends, his mother, sister, daughter, his friend's wives and his other female friends. He was constantly getting me to prove my love for him and every time he did something awful or disrespectful I'd forgive him and love him even more. He would give attention to other women to taunt me. It confused me so much to see how easily he could compliment, show affection and behave so lovingly towards other women. He made me beg for what he easily gave to them. I just didn't get it.

The madness of it all! Even 10-year-old Faye was in the game. She was frequently aggressively jealous, often behaving like a scorned lover. She scared me at times and when she stayed over I would always put the vacuum cleaner behind the bedroom door when we slept so I could hear if she decided to come in to our room. I was afraid of what might happen if she did.

On two occasions I'd woken up to find her standing at the side of the bed looking over me. I had visions of her cutting off all my hair. She gave me a black eye once by hitting me aggressively in the face with a plastic tube just because I was talking to her father and she wasn't getting the attention she wanted. Looking back at those times I can see that Paul was abusing all of us, playing one off against the other.

Paul even confronted his ex-girlfriends' partners and used threatening behaviour if they didn't do what he said. I remember telling Paul that who the ex-girlfriends went out with was none of his business but he told me he would decide and would make sure no one got near the mothers of his children. Was he keeping the way clear so he could step back in to their lives as and when he wanted?

Paul was a controller and a bully.

He was infatuated with himself and often spent long periods standing in front of the mirror flexing his muscles. He would ask me what I thought of them; if I thought he was good looking; what other women I knew thought of him. He needed constant reassurance. It was exhausting.

Paul often told me stories about his friends, what they got up to and their strange fetishes. Once he told me about a friend who was into dwarfism porn and foot fetish. I later discovered that he was talking about himself; he was testing me to see how I reacted.

Paul's porn addiction was out of control. He admitted masturbating every couple of hours, sometimes in excess of ten times per day. He said he couldn't help himself and that he'd got used to masturbating all day whilst in prison. This self-inflicted abuse caused him terrible pain and medical issues. He often got infections, had excessive bleeding and struggled to pass water because of the discomfort. Paul couldn't maintain a normal sex life. He needed variety. Variety he couldn't get from one person.

Everywhere we went he would try to get the attention of some woman or other. It didn't matter where we were, in the bank, the supermarket, a shop. Every moment of the day he was looking for validation from other women. He often got unwanted attention from their male companions but he would bully them into submission and they would back down. He was so disrespectful. He would just do whatever he wanted whenever he wanted with no regard for anyone else.

I noticed one day how Paul seemed to be constantly staring at everyone's feet. Not just women, but men too. I confronted him about it and he just laughed. He later admitted it. He said, "I think feet are cute." From that moment on it was like a relief for him. Paul didn't hide it in the slightest. His mother's, sisters', daughters', strangers', anyone's feet would do. If we were in a restaurant he would stretch his neck to look under the next table just to get a glimpse of some stranger's feet. Feet were like silver milk bottle tops are to a magpie; he was magnetically attracted to them.

On another occasion we went to a charity shop to drop off a few bags of clothing. He let me carry all the bags whilst he stood holding the door open. I noticed he was staring at a woman who was sitting down in the shop; he was flirting openly with her, eyeing her up and down. We came out of the shop and I wasn't happy. I said, "Why? Why do that? It's so embarrassing." He said, "I wasn't doing anything. I just liked her shoes and the way she was dressed."

I often felt offended when he became sexually excited over the sight of a stranger's feet and needed to adjust his trousers. In a strange way it was a change from the embarrassment of him staring deep into the eyes of strangers and the constant flirting games he would play with the ladies he met.

The constant staring wasn't just him appreciating beautiful women. It was much more than that; he was like a lion stalking his pray. His eyes were transfixed. They were cold and stone-like, focused only on his mission. I'd noticed this behaviour early in our relationship and it was painfully uncomfortable for me. He would stare at anyone who took his fancy, my friends, family, work colleagues and strangers, in a way that I find hard to describe. All I can say is it was like he was probing into their soul, reaching in deep for some kind of sign that they liked him. It was a prolonged stare that was both intimate and cold at the same time.

31

Paul would try to justify this behaviour by telling me that's how he was. "I like to work people out," he'd say.

He made me feel so anxious and uncomfortable. I couldn't understand how he could treat me so badly.

On a working weekend break with my friends he spent the entire time flirting and staring at one lady in the group. I felt my blood boil. Paul sat with his arm around her laughing loudly. He was trying to make me react. Although she was married she was clearly drawn in by him and loved the attention and he was enjoying every minute of it. She told me later that night she couldn't resist a 'pretty' face. He sat for ages staring at her like she was the only woman in the room, just as he had done with me and, in all probability, the many the women before me.

Paul often accompanied me to my workplace when I was doing training for the team. Many colleagues were women. "Perfect," he must of thought, "more targets to flirt with."

Paul would sit there flirting and messaging the women. (I later found out he'd slept with some of them.) Everyone in the room knew. It was obvious; he would keep turning around smiling at the women behind him. Paul often arranged to drive some of the women home after the meetings while I cleared away and chatted to the other members of the team. He would just pick up my car keys like they were his own and off they would go. I remember feeling annoyed but whenever I mentioned anything he would turn it around and say that he was only helping me, doing me a favour by driving my colleagues home. He said I had no need to be jealous and he had no interest in them. He'd do anything to drive my sports car, often taking a long route around town just so he could pose in it. Many people thought it was his car as he took many a 'selfie' posing with my car and posted them on social media bragging about how well he was doing for himself.

I never questioned him. But it hurt so much! I felt like a fool! The trouble was Paul would always tell me afterwards how much my colleagues liked him, that he was just being friendly, or that they were ugly and not his type. He said that I was being paranoid and he only had eyes for me. The truth was I'd seen his ex-girlfriends and there was no particular type, any shoe seemed to fit so to speak. Also I'd seen the women he flirted with; many weren't attractive in any way. Some even had a manly appearance.

Nothing was straightforward. He complicated everything to confuse me.

I started to question myself. I couldn't understand why he treated me so badly; all I wanted was his love. Every minute of the day I was focused on him and my desire to make his life better.

I often thought of leaving Paul but then would feel sorry for the children or he'd say something nice and draw me back in. Thinking about it, Paul was only nice to me when he wanted something.

Chapter Four

Busy, busy, busy. Trying to focus, in between organising my business, managing my home life and helping Paul with his life.

I got held up in rush hour traffic. I was on my way to a meeting but needed to make a quick visit to his parent's house to pick something up. I was sitting in the car on a very busy roundabout when I had an overwhelming urge to phone Jayne, a girl in my team. Don't ask me why; it was as though I was being told that I must call her. I quickly dialled her number. The phone rang. Jayne answered. "Are you coming to the meeting today?" I asked her. "No," Jayne replied. "I told Paul I couldn't make it when I spoke to him yesterday." "Funny!" I thought. "He didn't tell me that he'd spoken to Jayne."

I continued and told Jayne that Paul had gone to a friend's wedding and that I would have gone with him but we weren't together when the arrangements had been made. Jayne seemed frantic and said she would ring me back in five minutes.

I was on a tight schedule, nearly at Paul's parents' place when she phoned back. I took her call. "I'm sick of these men thinking they can do whatever they want. I've been seeing him for six months," Jayne told me. "We met on a dating site. I feel it's only fair you should know the truth."

I felt hurt, angry and devastated. I'd invested so much time and energy in the relationship with this man and his two children, trying to make their lives better, and that was how he repaid me.

I was in shock. The man I'd thought was my rock, my bodyguard and protector had been in the arms and the bed of another woman. I felt totally betrayed.

My head was spinning. "How could he do this to me?" I asked myself. Paul had told me he cared for me, that I was his guardian angel and the only one for him.

The remainder of my journey to his parents' house is a blur. I remember knocking on the door but then I was on my knees. I don't know how I got inside.

I told Paul's parents what had happened. They told me that if his lips were moving he was probably lying; he had been that way since he was a little boy. They said that he had never been faithful to anyone.

They knew him better than most and told me they didn't trust him and for a long time his mother hadn't wanted him anywhere near their house. They explained that on one visit he had stolen from them. After that they hadn't seen him for years until I arrived on the scene and helped him with his anger issues.

I went to my meeting and performed like a robot, relaying my notes. I did what I needed to but I couldn't wait for the meeting to end.

Then I drove home. It was one of the longest journeys of my life.

During the journey Jayne rang again to apologise for what had happened. I didn't blame her; she didn't know that Paul and I were in a relationship. Paul had lied to her too. He told her that I fancied him but said he wasn't interested in me.

Jayne and I chatted for ages, talking through all the details. I knew everything she said was true; he had treated us both in the same way and had said the same things to us – it seemed as though he had a script that he followed each time he spotted a new target. He'd said to Jayne they were only friends as he didn't feel ready for a relationship but when he did it would be with her. He used her for food and back rubs. He talked endlessly about all the hard times he'd had.

We both had been his therapists. Somehow he'd managed to keep us a secret from each other.

Wow this guy must be on top of the world by now. "How much attention does he need?" I thought.

Jayne was an attractive, professional woman in her mid-thirties. She had her own house, a fantastic job and a great lifestyle. Her hair was like black silk and she had striking, big eyes and was very slim with lovely long legs. She was stylish, wore fashionable clothes and had an air of affluence about her. She was warm, kind and fun loving.

Jayne and I chatted most nights for the next couple of weeks. I guess we were both trying to understand what had happened, trying to help each other get over the hurt inflicted by the man we thought cared only for us.

Jayne told me that Paul was ringing her each day but she wasn't answering out of respect for me. I didn't confront Paul about his infidelity; I just ignored him in the same way he had ignored me time and time again.

Then one day Paul rang from a number I didn't recognise. "Sorry, sorry, sorry. I don't know why," he said. "I'm an idiot, a wanker. Please just talk to me. I know you are hurting. I am too and I need to explain," he begged.

I was mad at him, numb from the pain, but I agreed to meet him that evening. I'd done an intense class at the gym earlier that day and felt nothing. I could have been in a boxing ring being beaten up by a professional fighter and felt nothing. Emotionally he had torn me apart.

What Paul said that night is a blur; empty promises no doubt? One thing I do remember is that he admitted that he had been unfaithful and promised he would never do it again, that he wanted me and that I'd done more for him than anyone else.

I agreed to continue seeing Paul but knew I needed to be stronger and keep my eyes open in future.

I'd never questioned a partner before but now I was watching his every move. I started to feel clingy and my confidence had taken a battering.

I told Paul to delete all his 'f buddies', as he called them, and all the prostitutes he knew from Facebook, social media and his phone. I found an album containing photographs of all the women he'd slept with on his visits to Thailand and put it in a skip outside his house. "No more, I'm not having it, if you want me you have to be faithful and I demand respect," I told him.

I also tried to stop his foot fetish behaviour and the staring competitions with other women. It was so humiliating especially when the women would start smiling and stare back.

His betrayal caused me so much emotional pain. I needed to find out why he did it! Why? Why? Why? Paul was the only one who could answer my questions but he always avoided them. He blamed me for being over sensitive and caused me to doubt my judgement and my sanity. Looking back that was all part of his plan. I never got answers for any of the questions that haunted me. I felt that I always had to prove myself; prove that I was good enough to be with him. This made me strive harder and harder to please him.

Only a couple of weeks after I'd agreed to continue seeing Paul he said, "You can't keep going on about it. It's making me ill, you are making me depressed." It was always about him. He was so focused on himself and his pain, how I made him feel by talking about his behaviour and the hurt he had inflicted on me was never recognised. He never acknowledged my feelings. "Was he not the one who was unfaithful to me?" I asked myself time and time again but my anguish gradually subsided and I started to feel sorry for him again.

Paul told me that he realised he'd made a big mistake and promised that he wouldn't do it again. "What else do I need to know?" I thought. He'd sucked me in again and I tried my hardest not to upset him. "After all, he's been through enough," I said to myself. "I need to let this go. I can't keep questioning him over and over again." I actually started to feel guilty for the pain that I was, apparently causing.

Paul played the victim. He started moping around, telling his family and friends how low he was, how he'd admitted he'd made a mistake. He claimed that I wasn't being very understanding and I was making him ill by constantly asking him questions.

He didn't know that Jayne and I had spoken to each other in great detail about him and his behaviour. Then one day she messaged me while were together to ask how I was. Paul quizzed me about the messages, who was I texting and what was I saying. I felt like I was being cross-examined in court.

At first I refused to tell him what he wanted to know. Paul was furious! I loved having power over him and felt that, at last, I was wearing the trousers. Eventually, I admitted I knew every detail of his relationship with Jayne; that she and I had spoken for hours discussing all the despicable details. I got great pleasure from explaining that Jayne had told me she couldn't understand why she continued to see him after the first time they had sex as she had seen bigger genitals on an 18 month old baby.

Although he knew his penis was tiny (he even called it his tiny mushroom), he couldn't help but ask me if it was really so small. I just smiled. I had power over him and he hated it.

Before I discovered that the small size of his penis was caused by years of steroid abuse I'd often thought it was my fault, that I wasn't exciting him, that I wasn't sexy enough. I'd always tried so hard to look good, my makeup, my hair, and my clothes. I always tried to look the way he liked. I loved wearing dresses at one time but he wanted me to wear jeans. "I'd like you to dress like my mates' wives," he once told me.

When we went out Paul was often bombarded with text messages from the wife of one of his friend's. One said, "You'd best not be out with that fucking bitch." That came from a person I'd never met and who knew nothing about me except what Paul had told her. I felt sick! So much aggression from someone who I'd never even spoken to, let alone met. I knew they often texted each other. I'd seen sweet messages from her, "Happy valentines babe," and similar. Paul would say it was a bit of a laugh, that it was just banter between friends. Yet another game I wasn't involved in. They also had many private chats. He'd sneak off somewhere to talk out of my earshot, tell me the calls were private and not to be so paranoid.

I found it strange that Paul would send sweet messages ending with lots of kisses to his female friends and yet his messages to me would often end in nothing more than a smiley face. Whenever I mentioned this Paul would say that I was paranoid, that his female friends were just mates and I had nothing to worry about.

Paul never answered my questions properly. He would frequently change the question and answer something completely unrelated to what I'd asked him. It was so confusing.

He would tell me he loved me but in the next breath would say he loved his ex-girlfriend more than he'd ever loved anyone; that he was still besotted with her and couldn't imagine feeling that way about anyone else. Then in the next breath he'd tell me he'd never felt anything for anyone or anything, that he didn't feel emotion. Paul would often make me question myself and wonder if I'd misheard what he said. All the mind games were exhausting.

I'll never forget going away for a short break with Paul. I felt it would be a fresh start, time out from all the stress, time to forget about what had happened with Jayne and the other women. I was so looking forward to the weekend staying at a nice spa hotel and having our meals prepared for us. On the day we arrived we were waiting in a queue and Paul looked at a young woman for at least a minute. While I was standing next to him like a spare part waiting for him to finish his flirtatious game I noticed that she made a play for him and he was beaming, delighted with the attention. This incident ruined the weekend for me and tormented me for many months.

The stress was incredible! I noticed my memory was getting worse by the day. I often couldn't remember what I'd had for breakfast that morning. My emotions were affected too. I knew I wasn't happy and that our relationship was dysfunctional but I felt trapped. He owed me so much by this point; I'd invested so much emotionally and financially. I didn't know where he ended and I began.

Still, I stuck to him like glue, being there for his every need and asking his opinion about everything. I felt like I couldn't make my own decisions and needed him to make them for me. There were times when I thought I was happy but deep down, I knew I was deluding myself and deserved so much more. I thought I was in control of my life but several months later I realised that I hadn't been, I'd been his puppet on a string.

Paul clearly had no empathy or emotion. When my grandma was dying Paul showed that the world revolved around him and only him. I knew my grandma hadn't much longer to live but Paul just didn't care, he was more interested in seeing his family. Even though I begged him to stay and comfort me during her final hours he refused and went off alone to see them. He was so emotionally cold towards me, never being there for me when I needed him. I remember getting very upset and feeling totally abandoned. That wasn't the first time Paul had put me at the bottom of the pile and made me feel insignificant.

It was like Paul enjoyed seeing me suffering or in pain. I would often catch him smirking if I was upset or something bad had happened to me, or someone I cared about.

Paul had no respect for my health or me. I remember he would often shout from the bathroom asking me to wipe his bottom. There were times when he would smoke in front of me although he knew that I have problems with my breathing and cigarette smoke made it worse.

He was so disrespectful. He would take my things without asking, damage my property and not bat an eyelid. He just didn't care about the things I'd worked so hard for. He would drive my car like a maniac saying, "It's a sports car. It needs to be driven this way." He caused over a £1,000 worth of damage in the first week after I picked it up. On another occasion Paul dropped my laptop while getting it out of the car and just left it in the road for me to pick up. There were so many times he damaged my things. When I mentioned his disregard for my property he often accused me of keeping a list of his wrong doings and would just say, "Stop going on." or "Why are you getting at me."

Paul was so reckless and wasteful with my cash, using and abusing everything I had. He was like a vacuum, sucking the life out of me. Everything that belonged to me now belonged to him. I belonged to him. I was his property. Paul told me I was like a faithful dog and would come back time and time again even though he was hurting me.

Paul manipulated and love bombed me to extract cash with regular trips to the bank, telling me he needed me and he needed my financial help to set him up in business. He would never take responsibility and blamed me for not growing his business fast enough. "Do you know what you are doing," he would say. "I'm trying. I'm trying everything I know. I don't know what else I can do," I'd reply. "It's not growing fast enough," he'd snarl. He would get so annoyed and his face would become distorted. He expected me to grow his business but wouldn't lift a finger to help.

I often felt an energy from him that told me to keep on the right side of him. Paul would withdraw intimacy to punish me for saying or doing something he didn't like. To be honest anything was an excuse for him to withdraw. He would often stonewall me completely and ignore me for days.

Sometimes I would go to bed before him and often I would wake to find him devouring my feet. In the morning when I asked what he had been doing he would laugh and say he wasn't aware of it and must have been asleep.

The foot fetish was mild by comparison to some of the unusual things he did. He found it entertaining to put his fingers under my top lip and rub my gums. Paul had poor toilet hygiene and rarely washed his hands after going to the bathroom so this drove me crazy. He did it deliberately as he knew I am very particular about cleanliness and hygiene.

I often woke up to find him having sex with me. One minute I'd be fast asleep and then I'd wake, as he was about to finish. I'm such a light sleeper so how he managed to get my pyjamas off is still a mystery. I often woke in the morning with intense stomach pain, barely able to walk to the bathroom. The cause is still a mystery.

Chapter Five

I lived on my nerves. I found my days were filled by doing
what Paul wanted to do, instead of what I needed to do. He
continually asked me to do things that benefitted him. Every
day there was something he would say or do to try to cause a
reaction in me. He was very subtle in the way he did it. We
lived his life.

Paul knew I was on his case over the emotional incest with
Faye and the way he neglected Belle but nothing changed.
He continued to phone Faye and talk to her like she was his
lover and he continued to have a complete disregard for
Belle. He annoyed me so much. Paul had admitted there
was no balance in the way he treated the children; Faye got
everything, all the attention and the gifts, whilst Belle got
nothing. I tried so hard to help him get the balance right but
without success. At times I felt my blood would boil. He'd
told me that Faye was more important than Belle and even
gave more child maintenance to the eldest child's mother;
Faye knew about that. She talked to her sister like
something she had picked up on her shoe. I desperately
wanted to help Paul to treat Belle properly and give her the
paternal love and attention she deserved.

Often, after he'd had a lengthy phone conversation with Faye
I would ask Paul if he was going to phone Belle too. He
would get annoyed and tell me to keep my nose out; he said
that it had nothing to do with me. Day after day it was
always Faye, the golden child, who got all the attention.

The anxiety I experienced was incredible. I felt uneasy all
day, every day. I lived on my nerves.

Paul would see a girl on the TV and tell me how stunning
she looked. Then in the next breath he would say how much

she looked like some girl he'd slept with during the time he'd been with me.

Paul continued to play his silly games, constantly eyeing up people's feet or maintaining excessive eye contact. Even in restaurants he would sit staring at someone's feet or into the eyes of some woman or other at the next table until she started to flirt with him. I'd ask Paul to respect me and tell him, "It's not nice. Please stop your games." He didn't care. He would do whatever he wanted whenever he wanted. I didn't realise at the time that I was enabling the game by staying with him and accepting his disrespectful behaviour.

Paul was a sex addict and could never get enough female attention. His addiction was out of control, the women, the porn. He was sexually numb and needed a lot of various types of stimulation to keep him feeling alive.

It got to a point where there wasn't a day went by without me crying in the bath or crying myself to sleep thinking over the events of the day and the chaos he'd created. Often, he ignored me for hours at a time unless he wanted me to do something for him. My emotions were all over the place.

I could see that my daughter hated Paul but she tolerated him because of her love for me. She could see how the dysfunctional life we had was destroying me. I hated myself at times when I saw how uncomfortable she was in his presence. I felt I was letting her down. I should have been setting a good example of how a relationship should work but I just couldn't break free. I can't explain why. It just wasn't possible. It was like being in thick sticky treacle and every time I tried to walk forward the treacle would grip my foot and suck me back in.

There were times when I set off in the car to go to one town and ended up in another, totally bewildered about how I'd got there. I'd have tears streaming down my face and be wondering what on earth was I doing with this man. There was so much confusion. I knew our relationship was so toxic yet I couldn't break free. I was like a fish; he'd throw a net into the water and, even knowing the consequences, I'd swim straight into it. No matter how much Paul hurt me I was always drawn to him.

I spent countless hours on the phone talking to my friends while he was at the gym. I'd tell them about all the dysfunction. Talking about him was taking over my life. I thought I was going crazy. I'm sure at times my friends must have thought so too.

I'd question, "Is his behaviour normal?" and search for answers on Google night after night. "Am I expecting too much of him?" "Is it me?" I continually questioned myself.

I felt uncomfortable in my own skin and hated the way I felt inside.

Often I'd be busy doing something and find myself with my hand in my mouth unaware that I was biting hard into my skin. I only realised what I was doing when I crunched into the bone or I was distracted; this self-harm seemed to relieve my emotional pain. When I did realise what I was doing I often got upset. I knew I was in so much emotional turmoil but I was unable to break free from the cause.

My motivation disappeared. I lost my drive, my zest for anything. All my focus was on him and I started to do less and less for myself. I often stayed in bed till lunchtime and did less and less work. Our lives were spent living his.

I needed an escape. The pain was unbearable. Normally I can take a drink or leave it, months can pass and I might only have one or two glasses of wine, it really doesn't bother me that much. But I often found myself thinking about turning to alcohol just to escape for a while, to numb the pain. Luckily those feelings only lasted about 2-3 weeks.

I went to speak to my doctor about everything that had been going on, the dysfunction, how much pain I was in, how I felt so unhappy, how I loved this man so much but also hated him for causing me so much anguish. My doctor offered me medication and counselling. I didn't like the thought of popping pills so decided to manage without medication and chose to look for support groups instead of waiting for 1 to 1 counselling.

Paul had used, abused and lied to me over and over again. He was like the pied piper. I was his number one follower. Me, a confident, successful woman was at the mercy of this evil man.

I felt like I was losing my mind.

Chapter Six

Every new day brought more anxiety. Every minute would revolve around him and his every whim.

We were on a merry go round. I wanted to get off but couldn't.

I knew Paul was a very selfish individual but it was much more than that; there were no limits to the pain he would deliberately cause. He had scant regard for anything or anyone. Although he was aware of the destruction he caused he didn't care.

Every word Paul spoke was a lie. He triangulated so many people into his dysfunction for his own entertainment.

Paul was so entitled; a control freak with a very shady past. He was above the law and was still involved with illegal activities. He'd set up a business selling illegal goods and often boasting about his bad behaviour. I also discovered that Paul was on a police register for abusive relationships (see Glossary, Clare's Law).

Paul told me many stories about the behaviour of his friends inside prison and about his past, including more than 80 burglaries. I felt uneasy and burdened by hearing those things, which were totally alien to me. Gradually it dawned on me that he was a con man and his sole intention was to extract as much as he could from me.

Paul did start to earn money by getting others to sell goods on his behalf. He kept all the profit for himself. I didn't like his dodgy dealings and insisted that he kept them away from my house. I didn't condone what he was doing and didn't want anything to do with it.

I said, "You can pay me back and contribute to the bills now you have some cash." He replied, "I need it and you have your own money." Previously he had always pushed me to share, it had always been that my money was his money. Now he had no intention of sharing, his money was his and his alone.

Throughout the relationship I'd paid for everything! He'd slowly and calculatingly persuaded me to spend my carefully saved reserves on him. He'd manipulated me into giving him everything he wanted. "I need it," Paul would say, taking me to the bank. "We're working together, we're a partnership aren't we?" He made me feel selfish and greedy when I tried to refuse and I always backed down and gave him everything he asked for. I discovered that he kept cash in rolls of 50 x £20 notes bundles of £1,000 stacked in fish finger boxes in the freezer in his flat; I guess it was mostly made up of the money he'd extracted from me.

When it was my birthday Paul said, "Let's buy you a watch." He paid for it out of those rolls of money - I'd paid for my own birthday present!

It was almost Christmas and I saw a ring in a jewellery shop. It was a ring that I'd previously seen and planned to buy for myself one day. Excitedly, I told Paul about the ring but explained I couldn't justify spending that amount on myself. "Take the money out of your account and I'll put it back by Christmas. I'll pay," he said.

My savings had dwindled to nothing by that time and I knew that if I paid for the ring I'd have very little left but, yet again, I believed him. "Yes," I thought, "Paul does love me. He's promised to pay me back. He can be nice to me at times."

I was happy, thinking maybe this was a sign of better things to come. I went to the jewellers and excitedly tried on the ring. "Yes, I'll have it," I said. The thought of having that ring on my finger brought a smile to my lips and I was confident that the money would be going back into my account. I knew Paul was a compulsive liar but this time I really believed him. Did he keep his promise? Did he ****!

Everything was a game to him. Paul always got found out eventually. He behaved like a mischievous child and just laughed when the truth came out.

His family, my family, my friends and me; we were all merely pawns on his chessboard. Who was he going to play next? Paul controlled us all.

Even when I was on the phone he needed attention and would interrupt my conversations. I struggled to concentrate on anything that didn't involve him. He even controlled my sleep by waking me in the early hours needing sex, food or chocolate. He controlled everything.

All the time my focus was totally on Paul and I'd not realised that I'd become so indoctrinated by him that I'd become an extension of him. I was his servant, his lover and his therapist. I was so torn; he took advantage of me so much but I always believed that I could help to make things better for him.

Paul often spoke about himself being at least two people; when he was being nice he would say that was him, one personality. Then when he was being awful he'd say that was the other Paul, his alter personality. He told me he constantly had a battle between the two personalities going on in his head. He said that he couldn't ever remember being happy. I felt so sad for him.

I've always been a caregiver; I love helping people and I just couldn't desert him. He seemed so helpless without me. But I could often hear my inner voice screaming out to me, telling me to get away from him, to protect myself. I was so lost by this point, so sad, that I'd joined him in the dysfunction of his dark world of pain.

Due to all the confusion my memory became badly affected I often couldn't even remember what I'd eaten that day.

Over a year after our relationship ended a friend of mine reminded me of the time Paul told me, for no reason at all and in front of a crowd of people, to "Shut the fuck up." I didn't remember the incident until I was reminded of it so I guess his terrible behaviour had become the norm and I just couldn't see what was going on. Looking back I can now recall Paul continually telling me to "Be quiet" and "Shut the f word up" and not to talk about his dysfunctional behaviours.

Chapter Seven.

In the final weeks more deceit emerged, more lies.

I frequently switched from feeling sorry for Paul to hating him. I was angry, angry about the way he took advantage of me, angry with myself because I'd become so focused on him that I'd forgotten about myself. The more I talked to friends and educated myself about narcissistic abuse the more I realised how bad my situation was; how calculating his scheme to extract everything he wanted from me had been. I eventually realised that my relationship with Paul was doomed but I clung on, not wanting to admit defeat.

I can now see clearly that he was slowly distancing himself from me during this period, making space between us in readiness for his departure from our relationship. He'd already had everything I could give him and I guess he was on the prowl for his next victim, someone with a new supply of everything he wanted.

Paul would try to convince me that I had got it wrong but his protests of innocence only made me become more and more vocal with my requests for him to meet my needs.

I continued to research narcissism. As I learnt, I became ever more aware that I was experiencing serious abuse which was severely affecting my mental health. I felt unloved, unwanted and used by him. I begged him to notice me, to make me feel that I was an important part of his life. I told him if we were to continue in a relationship we needed to see a therapist together and that I wanted him to repay the money that I had given to him.

I wanted to talk to the therapist to try to understand why he would, more often than not, only be intimate with me while I was asleep. I often wondered if he drugged me, as that would explain many things. I wondered why I had stomach pain so often and why I felt so tired and why I didn't wake up properly during sex. I also wanted to try to understand Paul's strange preferences; I'd caught him watching a video of someone standing over a girl and smacking her; she was tied up and gagged! That was very alien behaviour to me. It made me feel that I was inadequate in some way, that I wasn't good enough, but there was no way that I was going to allow myself to be subjected to that sort of treatment. When I tried to speak to him about it he said that it was private and none of my business. There were so many things that I felt weren't right and I wanted answers.

Paul eventually agreed to go to a therapist with me. He sat there, cool and collected, and brazenly claimed that it was entirely my fault, that he only went with other women because I nagged him. He even flirted with the therapist who was clearly drawn in by him and his advances. After two sessions with her I decided we weren't getting anywhere and it was time to stop his game. I realised if we continued it would just feed his endless need for attention and the therapy would only serve to develop his manipulative skills even more. I was sure that Paul would end up sleeping with the therapist too!

I had a work trip to Italy coming up. I thought that would be a great opportunity to try to mend our relationship. Before we embarked, I told Paul what I expected of him and emphasised that we couldn't continue as we were because it was so unhealthy. Paul was strangely attentive and loving while we were away and I thought maybe he had taken notice of what I'd said. But there was a free bar every evening and, as the trip progressed, he started drinking excessively. When we got home he told his family and friends he had relapsed into his addictions because I'd been so awful and abusive to him. I can now see that his drinking was a very controlled way of shifting blame on to me. Basically he didn't like me setting boundaries and expectations as I had done before we went away so he had decided to make me out to be the abusive one.

I realised Paul had always been a dry alcoholic and he had been swapping one addiction for another. He admitted to taking opium-based painkillers throughout our relationship. His family and friends were supporting his drug and alcohol abuse and he got into a very sorry state.

We list the people with whom we have experienced sexual conduct.	We ask ourselves what we did	We list the people with whom we have experienced sexual conduct.	We ask ourselves what we did
Kay	Used her & abused her lied to her	Best friends wife	Used her for sex then ignored her
JoAnn	Used her for sex and massages and food	Kay	Had sex with others without condoms then had sex with Kay
James	I beat him up	JoAnn	Used her for sex to meet my needs & lied to her
Faye	Lack of love & attention	Jayne	Used her for sex without protection & lied to her
Concetia	Verbal abuse for weeks	Toni	Used her for sex 1 night stands

Reproduction of Paul's Inventory

He turned back to NA (Narcotics Anonymous) for help. When an addict relapses and speaks with their sponsor they fill out a form called an inventory. I found Paul's under his bed. Among other things, he had admitted that he'd slept with other women while he was in the relationship with me, even his best mate's wife. He had no moral compass. He knew exactly what he had done and that it was wrong but his self-centred needs took over and prevented him from being a decent human being.

My friends asked me how I felt when I found Paul's inventory. I felt nothing! It was strange, as though I was emotionally dead. I couldn't feel the pain anymore. I guess he had hurt me so much there was nothing left to feel.

Admitting his wrong doings to his family and friends was a different matter. I found out that Paul had been bad mouthing me, making out I'd been abusing him. He turned into a most credible victim.

I reached for support from Al Anon, a support group for partners, family and friends of addicts. I fought desperately to find answers and often went to Al Anon meetings six or seven times a week.

Paul became more and more secretive and verbally abusive. I guess he must have upped the level of abuse as I really started to notice it - I think previously I must have been blind to it. He was so manipulative, controlling me with money, always making sure I was short of cash. When I mentioned that my money had gone he often told me to get another job!

On a few occasions, just a few weeks before he left, Paul kept saying, "It's not like we're together because my name isn't on your house."

"I paid the mortgage off ten years ago so I don't see any point in changing things now," I said. He persisted and persisted that it would be for the best if I transferred the house into joint names. Eventually I said, "Look, if it bothers you that much, I'll transfer the house into my daughter's names." Paul looked at me in total disgust.

From that moment I knew all he wanted was more of my money. That's all he wanted all along. My inner voice screamed, "You need to get out of this."

Paul had used me from the beginning, physically, emotionally and spiritually. Financially he wiped me out. He conned me out of more than £90,000.

Paul had used my business as a dating agency to get close to my colleagues and had taken advantage of everything and every opportunity.

It felt like my world had fallen apart.

Paul said, "We can stay together if you like but you need to keep your mouth shut." I knew I wouldn't be able to keep my mouth shut. Too much had happened between us. I knew that the relationship had to end but I felt I would die as I told him we couldn't stay together.

He moved out!

I didn't really understand what had happened but I knew breaking up was the only option. I had no energy and just cried myself to sleep for weeks and weeks barely leaving my house.

Many people may wonder how and why I continued to stay with this man for so long. Why, after so much upset, so much deceit and betrayal? Why would I stay?

The truth is I don't understand it myself. Paul worked his way into my heart and, despite everything, I didn't want to let him go. It's not just me; I've realised it's the same for thousands of other men and women in abusive relationships around the world.

It's been explained to me like this …

...If you put a frog in a pan of warm water he will swim around quite happily. Then if you turn up the heat under the pan very slowly the frog will get more comfortable and fall into a deep sleep unaware that he's in danger and eventually will boil to death.

A very similar thing happens in a narcissistic abusive relationship. These people are clever. Initially they seem unthreatening and can easily worm their way into your life. They build trust and respect and then the abusive, manipulative behaviour starts. Then, when they have got what they wanted, they dump you and move on to their next target. They are so clever and manipulative that they can often dupe the professionals into believing that they are the victim. They can even draw the professionals into having a relationship with them.

Being in a relationship with a narcissist or sociopath is so complex...nothing is black or white...

Chapter Eight

Paul has gone. "This is good," I told myself. "It's for the best. I know that!"

I honestly felt deep down that if we hadn't gone our separate ways I would have ended up in a box six feet underground.

My friend John reminded me of what I'd said many times during the chats we'd had. I'd said, "He's a shit load of problems, but I think I can help him."

How wrong I'd been.

The realisation that I'd only ever been a source of supply to him was so very painful.

I felt lonely, used, abused, angry, deserted and traumatised. The things that had happened, the things he had done, kept haunting me. I had no motivation. I didn't even want to get up and dressed in a morning. It was all so painful. I'd experienced emotional pain several times before I met Paul but those episodes were relatively mild compared to this.

The emotional pain manifested itself as physical pain. I felt wretched and for three months I could do little more than lie on my bed day after day ruminating over and over again. I couldn't get my head around how or why this could have happened to me. I'm well educated, have a good job, a nice home and good friends. I help so many other people who often come to me for advice.

How could I have let this happen to me?

During those first three months my thoughts revolved solely around Paul and the chaos that he'd brought into my life. I was going round and round in circles looking for answers and not finding any. Then my thoughts began to change and I started to focus on me again. That was the turning point! Once I started to think about me and the good things that remained in my life the emotional wounds started to heal.

But I didn't stop looking for answers!

I'd undertaken many years of therapy style training, studied counselling and phycology to increase my knowledge, mainly to get a better understanding of myself, but I thought I had a good understanding of people too.

How could this have happened to me?

I spent weeks researching, trying to understand what had happened, many hours searching on Google and listening to audible books online. I found a book called 'Should I Stay Or Should I Go, Surviving A Relationship With A Narcissist' by Ramani Durvasula. This helped me to realise that Paul was a narcissist. I did the test and crosschecked everything. There was no doubt about it.

Although Paul was out of my life I knew that I needed on-going support. I reached out to friends who understood. I continued going to support groups, Al Anon, CoDA (Co-Dependents Anonymous) and CoSA (Co-Dependents of Sex Addicts). I decided to learn everything I could about what had just happened to me.

I watched so many videos on YouTube, Ross Rosenberg (author of 'The Human Magnet Syndrome: Why We Love People Who Hurt Us), Melanie Tonia Evans (an expert in the field of narcissistic abuse recovery and self-empowerment) and many others.

I realised that, because I'd become so engrossed in Paul and forgotten about myself, I was suffering from 'self-love deficit disorder'. I desperately tried to overcome this by learning to love myself again.

I delved deep into my past with the help of my support groups and other people in recovery. I've learnt that I need to set boundaries in every relationship and protect myself, something I've struggled with in the past.

I've learnt to be my own best friend, to listen to my needs, my inner voice and to let my body tell me what it wants. Now, if something doesn't feel right, either I don't do it or I speak up. If I'm tired take a nap.

I've learnt to recognise that only I can look after me. I've learnt that I can't satisfy all my needs from external sources, some things - happiness, peace of mind, self-esteem etc, must come from within me.

Now, if I'm upset with something, I'm learning to sit with it, understand it, feel the pain and the emotion it evokes and let it out instead of bottling it up.

What the bullies did before I met Paul was inexcusable! What he did was inexcusable. Between them they bulldozed my life into a million pieces but now I'm in the process of picking them all up and putting them all back together. When I'm done I will be stronger than ever.

It won't be straightforward. In early 2016 I was diagnosed with PTSD – Post Traumatic Stress Disorder; it's been extremely debilitating at times. I've also experienced much physical pain and illness including a benign tumour and painful fibromyalgia caused, I believe, by the high levels of stress that Paul caused.

My emotions have been so erratic. I've experienced some very dark periods, spent many months hibernating at times not feeling able to see family or friends, not feeling able to leave the sanctuary of my home. But now I can see light at the end of the tunnel. The pieces of my life are starting to fall back into place and every day looks brighter.

While I've been writing this book I've recalled so many more details about the things Paul did and the way he treated me. There have been painful times as they have risen into my consciousness but now that I've faced them and dealt with them I can consign them to history.

Chapter Nine

After we parted it took me almost nine months to begin to understand what had happened to me. I knew on one level what had happened but I couldn't comprehend how or why someone could behave so badly towards another person, me.

I needed to understand why I attracted this insidious, Machiavellian man into my life and why I put up with his behaviour. I had to learn to to focus on me again and to recognise the good in my achievements and myself.

They say that everything happens for a reason and I now believe that I unconsciously attracted Paul to me to heal emotional traumas that occurred earlier in my life.

These were the keys to finding my sparkle again but it hasn't been easy.

Over a year after he left I was still experiencing the devastating aftermath of our insidious relationship. He and his 'flying monkeys' were still spreading untruths about me. ('Flying monkeys' is the term used to describe people who are used by the narcissist to back up their lies.) Paul is still trying to discredit me, all because I got him to see his true self, that he's a narcissistic sociopathic abuser.

After Paul left, his mother contacted me to tell me she was coming to my house to collect his things. I told her, "Don't bother. He's already had enough."

He's been in contact with many of my friends asking them to persuade me to contact him. I know that if I did he would try to manipulate me and attempt to draw me back into his web of dysfunction. He would use the classic one liner he uses to try to trap all his women, 'Can we just be friends'.

Basically this is a typical way for a narcissistic sociopath to keep several women on the go at the same time and use them as 'friend with benefits'. Paul himself had told me that when he split with his previous girlfriends that is what he did, remained friends and slept with them all. Of course he assured me it would be different with me but within days of us parting he went back to his default settings and added all his ex-girlfriends and prostitutes onto his social media again. I expected that but I didn't expect him to make friends with people who he had fallen out with in the past, people he told me he would beat to a pulp if they ever crossed his path again.

While we were together, Paul would often tell me to apologise to him for something he had done to me. I'd be heartbroken, really thinking I'd done something to hurt him when deep down I knew I had done no such thing. I knew nothing was wrong with me yet I got triangulated into half believing I was in the wrong. It was all part of his sick twisted game. Paul would even waken me in the night to tell me he deserved an apology. I'm sitting here now shaking my head in disbelief at how that man had me wrapped around his little finger.

When we split up I said I was sorry for anything I'd ever done to upset him. Looking back, I treated him like a king and helped him so much with every aspect of his life as he'd asked me to. Do I really have anything to apologise for? Definitely not!

Friends would point things out to me and say, "He's abusive. Why are you with him?" "It's a very complex situation," I would reply. Narcissistic abuse doesn't happen suddenly. It creeps in slowly, a purposeful, painful, dehumanising rape of your soul.

Looking back over my life I can now see that I've had several relationships with narcissists and sociopaths. "Why?" I hear you ask. It's because I'm a sensitive person and typically sensitive people draw narcissists and sociopaths to themselves like moths to a flame. It's all due to programming in our earlier years. Family members, caregivers, teachers; we learn a pattern of behaviour from them which leads us into broken, dysfunctional relationships with these people.

Whenever I met someone I've always thought that they would be warm and caring just like me, that they would think in the same way as I do. I've never suspected that they might have a hidden agenda. I've never learnt to take care of me. I've frequently abandoned myself and my needs and taken responsibility for other people and their needs. I've feared being abandoned and rejected and I've gone to great lengths to make others lives better. I've looked for love in the wrong places and been a magnet for people who play power and control games. In relationships I've been easy to manipulate due to my conditioning and my need to please. I've failed to set boundaries and given partners too much benefit of the doubt. I've not understood my value as a human being.

When we meet these devious people, we make it easy for them to be comfortable with us; for them it's like going home and putting on a comfortable pair of slippers. We are kind and caring. They are takers, selfish and unkind.

When you are in a relationship with a narcissist you wake up one day and realise you don't recognise who you've become. I knew my nerves were shattered. I was showing signs of emotional fragility. I became angry and fed up. This is quite common, it's all part of the narcissists plan to make you appear emotionally unstable so that their story will seem completely plausible if they need to discredit you later on.

When I finally came back into the land of the functioning I thought that, due to being so involved with Paul, I'd distanced myself from my daughter. I felt so very guilty. She assured me that I hadn't, that I had been there for her when she needed me. Thankfully we are now closer than ever and our relationship is going from strength to strength.

I know that my recovery starts with me looking at me. I need to be my own best friend. I've just started trauma therapy and CBT (Cognitive Behavioural Therapy) and I've started to put boundaries in place with everyone in my life so I know where I end and they begin.

Often other people think they know what's best for us and tell us so. That's part of the reason why we become so uncertain of ourselves, we struggle to take control of our lives because we are so used to others influencing our thoughts. The truth is we know ourselves better than anyone else. It's OK to listen to advice but in the end we must trust our own judgement, trust ourselves.

A friend said to me, "I wish you had never met him." I replied, "Yes me too, but maybe he's done me a favour. My eyes are open now. I can see so much more about people and their behaviour."

To this day, I regularly have nightmares about being conned, about Paul pinching my car, my money and breaking into my house. I often have dreams about being unable to protect people I care about. I wonder if it's my subconscious telling me I could never protect myself from him. I know once a narcissistic sociopathic person sets their mind on a target they will manipulate their victim until they get what they want. Paul certainly did that with me.

Paul, my narcissistic sociopathic ex-partner, is the most amazing liar I have ever met. The frightening thing is his lies sound so credible. He's had a lot of practise I guess. Like a chameleon changing colour to blend in with its surroundings, this type of person mimics other people's emotions so he can fit into their world. The scary thing is that as time passes and Paul gathers more followers he will develop more skills and can only get better and better at deceiving people.

Thinking about what happened, ruminating about it over and over and over, didn't resolve anything. It just made me ill. Narcissistic abuse isn't something you can get over quickly, it takes as long as it takes and it's important to process it fully. Reaching out for support to people who understand and have experienced this type of treatment, including going to CoSA and CoDA groups, was a huge part of my recovery.

I now meditate regularly, go for long walks and listen to my body. When I need to rest I find colour therapy is great for relaxation. Allowing my brain time out to relax by thinking about pleasant things definitely helps. Watching films and learning new skills have been lifesavers too.

I've learnt to focus on myself, listen to what my body needs, enjoy my own company and not commit to too many things at once. Now I just take one day at a time. I'm enjoying my freedom and new experiences. A now deceased family member told me to 'Have lots of fun'. I'm certainly fitting as much fun and laughter as I can into every single day.

I'm grateful for my family, good friends, the support network I've developed and my personal growth resulting from this experience. By far, this has been hardest lesson I've faced so far. On a spiritual level, I believe this experience didn't happen to me, it happened for me - to help me develop into a better human and spiritual being. I know that I'm a very different person now compared to the one who met Paul at that fateful business meeting.

In the early months on my own I couldn't stand the emotional pain that Paul had caused and I often thought that I would be better off dead. That's the truth of how debilitating narcissistic abuse is. At times I felt that I'd never be well again, that I was damaged so deeply that I'd never recover. It was a daily battle to remain positive.

At times the mental and emotional trauma that man put me through still makes me feel so very angry; angry beyond anything I previously could ever imagine. I often wish I could hear that he's been brutally murdered or tortured but then my compassion resurfaces and I hope that Paul will achieve peace of mind one day. I will continue to pray for him when I feel the need.

I had my heart ripped out and smashed into a million pieces but he's not broken my spirit! I'm still alive and I'm rapidly recovering. I have the determination to work hard, to restore my 'rainy day' fund and live a happy, fun-filled life.

I know that it's pointless for me to have another relationship at this point in my life and for me that's OK. This lesson has taught me so much but I'm still afraid that I would attract the same wrong type of person again. I'm still learning so for now I'm enjoying my own company, family time and time with friends.

I've often felt like posting snippets of my story on social media to tell the entire world about that man's despicable behaviour. But I haven't. Instead I decided it would be far more constructive for me to write this book to record the true, honest facts about what actually happened. Writing about my story has been great therapy and has helped my recovery so much. Committing the rawness of what actually happened to paper has been so liberating and I'm sure it will help me achieve closure for this traumatic time.

I sincerely hope that reading about my experience will help you, or someone you know, to see that you are not alone, to reach out for help and see that there is light at the end of the tunnel.

My sparkle is coming back stronger each day. If you've lost your sparkle I pray it will quickly return and brighten your life for many years to come.

Love and Healing

Kay x

P.S. Something to be aware of. Individuals can have narcissistic traits but that doesn't necessarily mean that they are a narcissist.

Over the years different types of narcissism have been identified and individuals can fall into one of many groups, for example: covert, overt, vulnerable, somatic, grandiose, malignant, cerebral and many more. You can find more information about these types in the highly recommended works of **Ross Rosenberg**, author of 'The Human Magnet Syndrome' and founder of 'The Self Love Recovery Institute'.

Also there are fabulous videos on YouTube by **Melanie Tonia Evans, Jerry Wise, Spartan Life Coach** and self proclaimed and twice diagnosed narcissist **Sam Vaknin**.

When An Empath Loves A Narcissist

There has never been a more toxic union, than the relationship between an empath and a narcissist.

An article by Raven Fon

Empaths often are misunderstood as being weak, or victims of their kindness. That's not the case at all. Empaths are strong, resilient individuals who are highly sensitive to the feelings and emotions of others. However, when narcissists enter the picture, "victims" are exactly what empaths become, if they don't know how to protect themselves and create boundaries.

Empaths want to heal the world, and can't stand to see someone in pain. Because of this, they are naturally drawn to the irreparably damaged narcissist and their tales of woe. But a narcissist doesn't want to heal - a narcissist wants to manipulate, belittle, and most of all, continue to be a narcissist.

Even though yes, most empaths are already aware that being in a relationship with a narcissist is an unhealthy decision, they might not know *exactly* what they are in for - until now.

Here are 17 things that happen when an empath loves a narcissist:

1. The narcissist creates a sense of comfort for the empath. An empath will feel a strong connection to the narcissist, even if he or she does nothing to reassure the empath that their feelings are correct.

2. Empaths love to love. They enjoy making other feel "whole" again. But there is a problem…the more love and care an empath gives, the more powerful and in control a narcissist becomes.

3. The narcissist will make the empath feel like the relationship is going well, but what is really happening is the narcissist is seeking constant validation. They ask, "You love me, right?" and swiftly turn any (and every) conversation into one about themselves.

4. After a while, the narcissist will begin to use "gaslighting" tactics to make the empath feel enormous self-doubt. "I never said that." "You're crazy." and "You're imagining things." are common phrases that start the rapid decline of an empath's mental stability.

5. This creates a relationship of control for the narcissist. They leave the empath feeling reliant on them for everything - they begin to feel like no one else would want them.

6. All of these manipulation tactics and control mechanisms cause many empaths to experience severe depression and anxiety. This only furthers the empath's belief that they "need" the narcissist in order to feel okay. They alienate themselves and the narcissist becomes their entire world.

7. Everything a narcissist says and does is a direct attack on your personal reality. They can take you from the joy and normality that you once had in your life, to a shadowy place where feelings of inadequacy and worthlessness are daily occurrences because *everything* you do is wrong.

8. At some stage in the relationship, the empath will reach their breaking point. The person they once were becomes someone else…and their friends and family no longer recognize them.

9. Conflict in the relationship arises between the empath and the narcissist because the empath starts to take on the traits of their partner. Eventually, they begin to realize that their emotional needs are not being met, and display actions that say "my needs matter too." The narcissist sees this as selfish behaviour.

10. What neither member of the relationship realises, is that even after it ends (which it will), both parties continue to suffer. The narcissist will continue on to other, equally toxic relationships, and pursue various avenues in their life - but they will still be miserable.

11. And the empath will continue experiencing the abuse from a narcissist because it works like a poison in their mind and body. It enters every cell with one purpose - to destroy the reality of their target.

12. After the relationship falls apart, the empath looks to themselves as the problem. Surely it is their fault - they must have failed in some way. All of the narcissist's toxic words come back to haunt the empath, and they think "maybe I *was* selfish for thinking about my own needs."

13. However, the empath doesn't realise something very important - there is nothing wrong with them, and they didn't "fail" anything or anyone. In fact, there is something very right with them. They simply were manipulated, used and lied to by someone who had no remorse about hurting another individual.

14. This begins the empaths powerful transformation. It is a painful process, but so is being with a narcissist. They begin to understand that in order to grow, they must re-evaluate their "healing" process. Everyone is worthy of love, but not everyone is deserving of trust.

15. The empath *will* heal. It takes a realisation that they too were broken and damaged, like the narcissist, but they are willing to recognise that - whereas the narcissist simply refuses to believe they could possibly be flawed or in need of anything (or anyone).

16. The narcissist will carry on, looking for their next victim, completely unaware that their unhappiness is caused by themselves.

17. The empath will grow from this experience, and recognise that they must protect, and balance themselves if they are to live a wiser, more enriched life.

Raven Fon is a freelance writer and a globetrotting journalist. She studied creative writing and journalism at Saint Petersburg College and has since been a contributor to several written and online publications including her own MysticalRaven.com.

Glossary

Clare's Law – otherwise known as the Domestic Violence Disclosure Scheme gives members of the public a formal mechanism to make enquiries about an individual who they are in a relationship with, or who is in a relationship with someone they know, where there is a concern that the individual may be violent towards their partner.

Co-dependency – Co-dependents are honest, kind, caring people. They often form relationships that are one sided and emotionally destructive with self-centred, abusive controlling partners.

Problems with co-dependency occur when someone represses their emotions and disregards their own feelings or needs.

The person becomes focused on their partner's needs above their own.

Flying Monkey – This is a term often used for people who act on behalf of the abuser, supporting them in their abuse of another person.

- Flying monkey side with the abuser to enable social, financial or emotional abuse.

- Flying monkeys are used by the abuser to relay hurtful, intimidating or trigger messages to their target.

- Flying monkeys are loyal supporters of the abuser as they have been fed a web of lies about the target.

- Flying monkeys spread false rumours with a bit of truth mixed in to make the story more plausible.

- The abuser uses smoke and mirrors to deflect attention away from their dysfunctional behaviours.

Gas Lighting – This is a form of brain washing which makes us doubt our own mind, memory and perception.

- The abuser will manipulate you to get a reaction. When you react the abuser will make you feel like you are crazy by make you feel like your reaction to their abuse is irrational.

- The abuser will deny facts and events and provide you with false information making you doubt your own mind and become anxious and confused. It is an emotional form of abuse and manipulation and over time will no longer trust your senses, skills, family or friends.

- The abuser will swear the sky is black when it's clearly blue but they will get so deep into our heads we start to doubt ourselves.

Love Bombing – refers to constant communication and compliments from the abuser when they first meet you.

- They are 100% into you. They can't get enough of you. They rush intimacy. Constant text messages, phone calls, emails. Too much contact much too soon.

- They bombard you in this way because they want you will affirm your feelings for them. Then they know… they have you!

Narc – This is an abbreviation for a Narcissist.

Narcissist – This is a person with a personality disorder. There are many different types of narcissist's.

- A narcissist is someone who targets people who have something to offer them.

- He or she will trick you into a relationship with them by pretending to be everything you want. They weigh up how they can use you, emotionally, spiritually and financially.

- They are expert's in telling lies and masters of manipulation whilst also chronic pathological liars.

- They mimic emotions from an early age but in reality, feel nothing.

- They are unable to feel remorse, guilt or love but they are excellent actors and will convince you of their pain.

- They charm their way into your life with the sole intent of taking from you, giving you only sorrow and pain in return.

- They often come across as lovely people until the mask slips and you're no longer needed to inflate their ego. This is when they will move on to their next supply.

- They con, cheat and form fake relationships just to get what they want and don't stop until they get it.

- They are filled with a grandiose sense of self-importance. They are arrogant and entitled with a need for admiration or attention. They have problems with empathy. They act selfishly and they are often unfaithful and dishonest.

- They think they are better looking, smarter and more important than others and have an over-inflated view of themselves.

- They use others to achieve what they want. This is commonly known as narcissistic supply.

- With a narcissist, there's no problem. They can do whatever they want. There's only a problem if their abuse upsets you.

- They are abusers. They target selfless individuals to use and control them to satisfy their own needs. The target is usually a kind, giving person who is in control of their lives, often with a nice lifestyle and a good job. Many doctors and professionals have also been conned by these people.

- Some narcissists, target strong people just to gain control and bring them down. Some only target people they perceive as weak or vulnerable. Either way, these people will delve into your life and find your insecurities. If you don't have any they will create chaos to ensure you do, then traumatise you with it.

- If you need their support they won't give it, they will turn things around so that they are the ones who need the support.

- All your focus goes onto them.

- They make you doubt yourself.

- They need loving, sensitive, capable individuals who can mop up their mess.

- Once you show narcissists themselves in the mirror they will become aggressive and make you feel like you are crazy. They will always project their crap onto you by accusing you of the things they are often doing themselves.

- If you uncover them for who they are you will be at risk.

- Expose them and they will ruin you.

- They need a supply upon which to offload their tormented self.

- It's believed genetics and environment issues cause narcissism. Dysfunctional or abusive treatment in early years is also a possible cause.

- If you meet a narcissist I suggest you run and don't look back, otherwise it's the end of your life as you know it.

Paul was at the top of the narcissism scale with this mental disorder. Looking back it is now easy to see how calculating he was. Many narcissists are much more subtle and first thing you may notice is how they like to control you.

Narcopath – A narcopath is someone who shows all the signs of being both a narcissist and a sociopath. These people have no moral compass.

PTSD – Post Traumatic Stress Disorder. - PTSD is a mental disorder that develops after a traumatic event, often after narcissistic and sociopathic abuse.

It can include flashbacks of abuse, nightmares, anxiety, memory loss, low mood, depression, emotional numbness, difficulty sleeping, lack of concentration, ruminating excessively about what happened, avoidance of people and places and many other problems.

For many, PTSD can last for years.

Red Flags – These are signs or clues that something isn't right and there may be a problem just around the corner.

Sociopath – A person who disregards or violates of the rights of others.

- He or she can often be spotted by their ability to maintain eye contact, much longer than the rest of the population. It's often been referred to as the predatory stare.
- Sociopaths show a lack of regret for their wrong doings.
- Sociopaths have a total disregard for the physical and sexual wellbeing of others.

- Physical aggression is often a visible symptom.

- Sociopaths don't care what others think often getting into trouble with the law.

They are emotionally, mentally, physically, spiritually and often financially destructive.

Printed in Great Britain
by Amazon